10 Gifts

TO GIVE YOURSELF
The Journey Back to You

Sheryl L.W. Barnes

ww
WISDOM WORD PUBLICATIONS

Copyright © 2014
by Sheryl L.W. Barnes
All rights reserved
Printed in the United States of America

ISBN: 978-0-9748629-1-0

Published by Wisdom Word Publications
A DIVISION OF

Sterling-Xavier Consulting Group, LLC
P.O. Box 3605
Woodbridge, Connecticut 06525

www.sterling-xavier.com

Unless otherwise noted Scripture quotations are from the *New King James Version* of the Bible Copyright © 1979, 1980, 1982, Thomas Nelson, Inc.
All rights reserved.

> It is illegal and a violation of Christian ethics and principles to reproduce any part of this Copyrighted Book without the permission of the author or publishers.
> **Sheryl L.W. Barnes**

DEDICATION

To my husband, Linwood E. Barnes, who encourages me, provides for me, and prays for me; to my wonderful family; and to all who will read this book and decide to give themselves
10 GIFTS
for the journey back to themselves!

TABLE OF CONTENTS

INTRODUCTION …………………………......……7

How Did You Get So Far Away From You?..………....9

- What took you away from yourself?
- What is it costing you?
- Could you have said 'No'?
- What are you worth?
- If only? … *or*… What if?

Gift #1 - The Gift of Self-Acceptance………………..…25

Gift #2 - The Gift of Forgiveness……………….……….30

Gift #3 - The Gift of Healing………...……………..…..35

Gift #4 - The Gift of Self-Discovery………......………..47

Gift #5 - The Gift of Self-Affirmation……………….…55

Gift #6 - The Gift of Self-Development……………….60

Gift #7 - The Gift of Conscious Choosing……………..65

Gift #8 - The Gift of Self-Nurturing …………………71

Gift #9 - The Gift of Self-Love………………………77

Gift #10 - The Gift of Balance………..……………..82

Starting Here – Starting Now……..…………………..91
- Are you ready and willing to choose something different?

ABOUT THE AUTHOR………………………………..94

....

INTRODUCTION

Dear Friend,

I am delighted that you are reading this at this very moment because chances are, like many of us, you have given *too much* of yourself away. We serve a God who knows all things and who, in His wisdom, has ordained a life of trust in Him that brings freedom from worry, grace and mercy, restoration, and rest. Unfortunately too many of His children lug around the baggage of this fallen world into their covenant relationship and try to *earn* a place of acceptance, honor and appreciation when in reality they are **already** loved, accepted, honored and deeply valued by Him. That takes care of your spiritual value. But what about your value - socially or culturally?

In most western cultures (and these days, some eastern cultures as well) a great deal of value is placed on 'doing' that almost always comes at the expense of simply 'being.' If your way of thinking is set on autopilot as a result of the cultural norms you grew up with, you may not even *fully* realize that there are other ways of viewing and valuing your life.

This book was written to encourage you to pause and gently examine your choices, activities, expectations and…

your 'doing'. You are NOT your roles. You are NOT your titles, degrees, or job. Beloved you are not even what others think of you. So the question is who are you really and how did you get so far from you?

My goals for writing this book are three-fold: (1) To encourage you to explore how you got where you are; (2) To have you add up the spiritual, physical and emotional costs; and (3) To encourage you to consider and choose some new options. In pursuit of those goals I have three questions for you:

1. What took you away from yourself?
2. What is it costing you?
3. Are you ready and willing to choose something different?

After we've worked thru these three questions I will share **10 GIFTS** to give yourself with the hope that you will open each and every one and present it to yourself as a part of the journey back to the sacred placed called *you*.

It's time for you to take a much needed, and probably long-overdue, journey back to self. Every step of the way I will be cheering you on!

Let the journey begin!
Sheryl
Dr. Sheryl L.W. Barnes

How Did You Get So Far Away From YOU?

The title of this book implies "movement away" from yourself. Did you know that "movement" may be voluntary or involuntary? There are many decisions, behaviors, habits and actions which we take that are voluntary because we are motivated by love and caring for others. We often help others because, in the deepest part of our heart, we *want* to. We want to ease their suffering or discomfort. We want to stand with them in their grieving or misfortune. Years ago, as a mom, it never felt like a burden to run into my child's room when I heard him crying from a nightmare. It was a joy to comfort him! I'd sit with him until he peacefully fell back asleep. Likewise I have honestly enjoyed picking up senior citizen friends of mine to take them to lunch, doctor's appointments or to mid-week church services. Those were voluntary, conscious choices I made from my heart.

But there have also been times when I worked late into the evening because it was 'mandatory' and I needed to keep my job. There was a physical and emotional cost to putting in the extra hours and because I was 'salaried' there was absolutely no financial reward. When this recurred for weeks at a time it became taxing and stressful; it definitely was an involuntary movement away from a peaceful and healthy self.

Voluntarily or involuntarily sometimes we simply give *too much* of ourselves away.

I'm sure you have your own list of things you've done, and may still do, that bring you as much pleasure as the people for whom it's done. That's part of what makes us feel alive within our various circles of family, work, community and faith. Most of us would be utterly distraught if we were permanently isolated from everyone else on the planet. So, we get it. We understand that we "give ourselves away" because we choose to. In other words, in *most* cases, it is a series of *voluntary* actions we lovingly take.

But what about the ways in which we simply go… too… far? We look up and realize that everyone else's needs have been met and we are no longer on our own list? Can we talk about *that*?

What took you away from yourself?

Take a moment and really think about the question. Tell the truth as you compose your answer. What was it? Over-volunteering - because others know that when you give your word you will honor it? Have others begun to take advantage of you by manipulating you into service saying things like: "Nobody can put together an event like you; you are the first person we thought of!" Did you fall for that one *again* and somehow end up rationalizing your over-volunteering by telling yourself: "How can I say 'no' to such a worthy organization?"

Have you trained people to misuse you? Even when you didn't feel up to hosting Thanksgiving last year (because of your surgery, financial set-back, or whatever) family members started 'fast-talking' you saying things like "You don't have to cook – we'll help you" which everybody knew meant, including the ones who said it, **you** would have to clean the house alone, buy all the food, prepare it, decorate, set the table, *and* clean up afterwards!

What are some specific things that move us away from ourselves?

Here's *my* short list but please feel free to add other things to it as well:

- Hollywood images: depictions of perfectly-dressed, beautiful people in elegant cars, playing tennis, who seem to have it all!
- Culture: unfair roles or pressure to exhibit abilities that represent the cultural norms handed down thru time
- Traditions: always doing things because "it's our tradition" whether the things are reasonable or not
- Family expectations: such as the oldest child hosts out-of-town guests or the responsible sibling who works a steady job has to contribute more money than others
- Media: wear this, drive that, drink this, buy these, own this, follow us, repost that, like them
- Advertisers: a really *good* mom cleans her toilet with Brand X; a really *good* father takes his kids to Brand X theme park!
- The world's definitions of beauty, success, fulfilment, love, marriage, and etc.
- Perfectionism: unless you are scoring 100% everywhere in your life you are a disappointment or a failure
- Legalism (in the church): trying to keep the 'law' instead of accepting and flowing in grace
- Titles: being tricked into believing that lofty titles make you more valuable
- Professional or Career demands: overtime, double-time and triple-time are more important than good health and a sound mind
- Self-imposed judgmentalism: never believing the good things about yourself; not being able to enjoy a genuine compliment!
- YOU fill in the blanks…
- _____
- _____

What is it costing you?

When you look at the long list of what took you away from yourself do you have any idea of how much the true cost is to you? Do you know whether or not you have run up a tab that you can't pay - emotionally, psychologically, or mentally? Are you nearing an NSF (insufficient funds) situation as it relates to your well-being or is it much worse than that as in on the verge of filing an energy-bankruptcy?

Are you aware of your feelings or are you so busy getting things done, moving through life, meeting others' needs that you haven't checked in on your own emotions in a while now.

Beloved, when a friend asks "How are you feeling?" and you respond: "I'm tired," warning bells should be going off in your heart because *fatigue is not an emotion*; it is a state.

Have you ever started (or ended) a busy day feeling as if you were somehow on a rollercoaster, or even more disturbing, on one of those little wheels you see gerbils run on inside of their pet cage? I sure have. Ever been exhausted psychologically at the *beginning* of a day – dreading what was before you? If the mere thought of your day depresses and depletes you – something is wrong.

Let's talk about the costs of living like this. Do any of the following sound familiar to you? This is what you can wind up with after paying the exorbitant costs of giving *too much* of yourself away:

- Lack of joy
- High blood pressure
- Self-doubt
- Mental strain
- Sadness, depression or grief
- Cynicism
- Sarcasm
- Martyrdom
- Increased victimization
- Wounds that don't heal
- Stunted personal growth
- Hopelessness
- Self-sabotage
- Self-abuse
- Warped self-perception
- Jealousy & envy
- Skewed reality (life hurts)
- Apathy
- Low self-esteem
- Suspicion

What else is on *your* list? Have you stopped dreaming about a better life? Have you started believing that every day is going to be just like the previous day? Tell the truth.

When you give *too much* of yourself away you don't have enough left to properly nurture yourself: your dreams, your aspirations, your gifts and abilities. There simply is not enough left in your spiritual, emotional and psychological fuel tank to care for yourself. You are on empty. And it shows. And it matters – because YOU matter.

Beloved, let me share something with you at this point. If you took your time, went deep and really answered the last two questions: "What took you away from yourself?" and "What is it costing you?" I want to commend you because this is demanding work! It takes real energy to examine your own life and tell the truth. I have often engaged in such self-reflection and found myself unable to go to the 'next' activity, exercise or chapter before resting. I literally had to stop and wait a day before resuming the process.

There is something powerful and energy-consuming about looking into the recesses and secret rooms, closets and drawers of our *own* hearts. We can fake-out others; have them believing that we have it all together. After-all, we wear the right outfits, drive the right cars, hold the right degrees and attend the right church. We smile on cue. We host cool parties and laugh at the right jokes at the right time. But... when there is no one around to impress... when we sit alone with the truth of what we have made our lives into... wow... that's another whole kind of experience. What is my point? Simply this – take your sweet time as you read this book. *Feel* your answers to the questions. Walk around the choices you have made. Ask yourself why. Why did you do it that way – for that long? Just ask and then... answer. Do not belittle yourself or your choices. That is not what this is about. This is about compassionate inner-exploration because all of the real work one does in life begins inside of them.

This journey back to you has to begin in you and you **must** know how you strayed so far away from a balanced, self-loving, self-affirming, and self-nurturing lifestyle. If you are not able to sit compassionately with the you who gave too much of herself or himself away you will not be able to compassionately lead that same you back home. Selah* *(*Pause and think about it)*.

> REFLECTION OPTION: Pause here in your reading and do something kind for yourself. Prepare a cup of tea and drink it mindfully. Feel the warmth of the cup in your hands. Smell the fragrance of the tea leaves (or coffee beans or hot chocolate). Sip it slowly and enjoy the taste. Do not gulp. Put on music that you love. Try to imagine the joy the artist felt in producing such amazing music. Let each note and chord dance across your eardrum and each rhythm caress your heart; feel the

music. Now begin the journey from a place of self-kindness…

Are you ready to continue? Good.

Could you have said NO?

Take a moment to think of two or three instances when you gave *too much* of yourself away. List them but skip a few lines so that you can write something beneath each example of *over*-giving. Okay, now that you have real-life examples of how you gave *too much* of yourself away write, beneath each example, what it ***cost*** you. Be clear, be truthful. Here are three examples to show you how to analyze what you may have done:

1. I agreed to babysit at the last minute even though it wasn't an emergency.
2. I said 'yes' to chairing the corporate strategic planning retreat even though I've chaired it the last three years and we were supposed to rotate the chairmanship.
3. I accepted an invitation to three events on the same Saturday even though I'd really like to sleep late, garden, or head up to the beach. Not even sure how to attend all three since their times slightly overlap!

Next: beside each instance of giving *too much* of yourself away make a checkmark (✓) if you could you have said '**NO**'…

1. I agreed to babysit at the last minute even though it wasn't an emergency. ✓

2. I said 'yes' to chairing the corporate strategic planning retreat even though I've chaired it the last three years and we were supposed to rotate the chairmanship. ✓

3. I accepted an invitation to three events on the same Saturday even though I'd really like to sleep late, garden, or head up to the beach. Not even sure how to attend all three since their times slightly overlap! ✓

Last part of this reflection is for you to answer this question for each example you selected: "Have you done this before, in other words is this a habit or pattern for you?" Write **Y** for yes or **N** for no:

1. I agreed to babysit at the last minute even though it wasn't an emergency. ✓ **Y**

2. I said 'yes' to chairing the corporate strategic planning retreat even though I've chaired it the last three years and we were supposed to rotate the chairmanship. ✓ **Y**

3. I accepted an invitation to three events on the same Saturday even though I'd really like to sleep late, garden, or head up to the beach. Not even sure how to attend all three since their times slightly overlap! ✓ **Y**

What do you see? Is it a **habit** for you to say 'yes' to social commitments, hosting family gatherings, picking up friends from the airport, babysitting nieces, nephews, godchildren or grandchildren without checking your own calendar first? Have you developed a **pattern** of over-committing at work or church or in your sorority/fraternity, civic group, etc.?

When did your time, energy, rest, or resources become worthless to you simply because someone else valued their life *more* than yours?

What are you worth?

What are you worth in your own system of placing a value on things? What is your measuring device?

If I tried to convince you that pencils at your local dollar store were suddenly worth a few thousand dollars each and a new car over at the reputable dealership was somehow suddenly available for a couple of bucks you would, hopefully, be suspicious. Either something was wrong with the car or something was wrong with the dealership or something was wrong with me. New cars don't sell for a couple of bucks and pencils don't command thousands of dollars at the neighborhood dollar store. Exactly. Your time, energy, vision, knowledge, abilities, dreams and so on are not cheap commodities that others have a right to attach a ridiculously low value to. Neither should you.

Several years ago there was a movie out in which a man offered a married couple a million dollars in exchange for the chance to sleep with the married man's wife. When I taught college philosophy I would use this example to lead my students into a discussion about how we attach value to one another and relationships. I would write several currency amounts on the board, such as: $ 67.00, $ .52, $ 113.00, $ 600,000 and so on. I'd ask my students how much money they would accept in exchange for their spouse or significant other. Just about every student was outraged and insulted by the 52 cents figure and the discussions would get more intense as the currency values increased.

Who decides *your* value... society, your parents, the culture, employers, in-laws, significant other, you... or God?

The truth is that you are a divine expression of a holy God. You are unique. Fearfully and wonderfully made, according to Scriptures:

I will praise thee; for I am fearfully and wonderfully made: marvellous are *thy works; and* that *my soul knoweth right well.* Psalm 139:14 *(KJV)*

There is not, has not, nor will there ever be another person identical to you. You are rare and therefore priceless. Essentially, you *are* spirit. You *have* a soul (mind, will, emotions) and you *reside in* a body. My favorite way of explaining my own existence is that I am a spirit who has been given stewardship (management) over my soul and body. I don't own myself but I do have stewardship responsibilities. Since I do not own myself I do not have the last say as to my value – my Creator does. **He says** that I am His masterpiece:

For we are God's masterpiece. He has created us anew in Christ Jesus, so we can do the good things he planned for us long ago. Ephesians 2:10 *(NLT)*

Let's talk about what ***you say***. Complete this sentence: "I am valuable because_____."
Are you valuable because…
    … your spouse has an MBA?
    … you graduated from an Ivy League college?
    … you own your own home?
    … you live in a particular section of town.
    … you vacation in Maui or Martha's Vineyard or the Greek Isles?
    … you wear designer clothes and carry a platinum credit card?
    … blah, blah, blah, ad nausea?

You get my point. Notice the thread. All of the values are externally based, material and temporal. They aren't really the essence of you nor do they identify your essential value. Somebody lied and we fell for it.

If only?... or...What if?

If only you sported the latest purse or donned the trendiest suit. *If only* you were invited to the right, summer White Parties (where all the guests wear white) and your name was always on the A List. *If only* people dropped *your* name and folks followed you on Twitter. Really?

If only you were smarter, cuter, richer, thinner, wittier, better-known and better connected socially. *If only* money were no object and you never got sick. *If only* no one you loved left you or betrayed you or abandoned you.

But *what if* we replaced "If only" with "What if?" and took that concept for a spin. *What if* you are enough? *What if* you really are the Imago Dei (the image of God); His most prized creation with so many of His attributes? *What if* you are already amazing; full of gifts, covered by both grace and mercy and destined for unimaginable and incalculable greatness? *What if* your value is forever established by your heavenly Creator and His immutable excellence... then what?

If you are still reading I applaud you. Why? Because you've done some thoughtful introspection and now we can lovingly open up **10 GIFTS** and, from a place of gratitude and spiritual awareness, give ourselves permission to **receive** each one. My close friends know that I have a real problem with the popular concept of "going to *get* blessings." I honestly believe that blessings are gifts that manifest as we allow our faith to lead us into trusting and obeying God. We don't need to hustle-up on blessings. There is no scarcity in the spiritual realm. We simply need to re-train ourselves to *receive* what has already been given.

In our fast-paced, break-neck, 'hurry-up and get' culture we miss so much because we are moving so fast. We are also very challenged when it comes to being in the present moment. Someone recently asked me how she should be a good mom to her newborn child. My answer was for her to see if she could be a good mom for the next 10 seconds. She laughed and was quite confident that she could do that. So I told her to do another 10 seconds after the first 10 seconds had elapsed and she would discover for herself that parenting is really *in the moment*. When the baby is wet, change her. When she is alert and awake, sing to her and engage her. When she is frightened, hold and console her. And... ask the Lord for wisdom every day for the rest of your life because parenting requires wisdom in each moment!

I am about to share **10 GIFTS** with you and I'd like to first encourage you to do the same thing as the advice I gave to a new mom. Find your place of peace and in increments of 10 seconds at a time begin to be kind and compassionate to yourself. No more name-calling. No more comparisons (good or bad). No more vanity and no more self-loathing. You were hand-crafted by God and it is His breath that is in your body this very moment. Inhale. Now exhale. That's His breath in you.

I don't know if your mother of father "planned" you but God certainly did. He knew you before your parents knew themselves. He has also placed destiny in your heart and has phenomenal plans for you.

> *For I know the thoughts that I think toward you, saith the LORD, thoughts of peace, and not of evil, to give you an expected end.* Jeremiah 29:11 - *(KJV)*

Inhale. Now exhale. Inhale again. God's masterpiece is alive and breathing! Now… let's open some **GIFTS**.

#1 – The GIFT of SELF-ACCEPTANCE

When you gaze into a mirror, who looks back at you? Do you know her? Do you like him? Is she your friend or do you just tolerate her? Are you bothered by his faults and shortcomings? Do you accept who you are?

Open **The Gift of Self-Acceptance** first. In *this* moment accept everything about you; every victory and, yes, even every defeat. Every good thing you've done and every mistake you've ever made. Own all of it. Admit that you are still here… for a reason.

Accept your physical characteristics: your height, weight and breadth. Accept your build, your frame, your shape and all of your unique features. If you have any scars or physical bruises, accept them too. You are still here.

How many times have you heard family members make comments about your looks that made you self-conscious or sad? "Funny looking ears; feet too big; knock-kneed; bird legs; big hips; nappy head; stringy hair; beak nose; big lips;

boney; pale; dark!" Yes, there were probably many compliments along the way but somehow the comments that criticized and belittled us stung so much we could hardly remember the positive ones. Truth is you didn't pick your genetic composition. How far apart or close together your eyes are was not a decision you got to weigh in on. It's time to let it all go.

Accept that the God of the universe loves diversity. There are literally hundreds and hundreds of different kinds of flowers, fish, butterflies, plants and insects. The natural world proves how very much God loves diversity.

Self-acceptance is an often overlooked and under-valued form of power. The moment you begin to resist the opinions and judgments of everyone outside of yourself you reposition yourself as caregiver of your own soul. If you want to change anything about yourself do not do it until you first tell yourself "I accept me!" and really mean it.

Accept your personality and temperament. I am an introvert and have, for the majority of my life, *wished* I was an extrovert. After years of 'wishing' guess what? I am still an introvert. I am actually energized by being alone or in very small groups of people. After I earned my Bachelor of Arts degree in psychology from The University of Michigan I went on to earn four more degrees (a Masters and three

Doctorates) all of them working *alone*. Hours upon hours of studying things that brought me immense pleasure from quantum physics to philosophy to theology – I studied by myself and wrote a thesis and three doctoral projects. I am not weird. I am an introvert and it is very common for introverts to enjoy self-directed study.

What is it about your temperament or personality that others *thought* needed fixing when in truth was never broken, simply different from them? Name it and then accept it.

Accept your natural talents as well as your spiritual gifts. Your natural talents are those abilities that you were born with. I love being around and observing children because they demonstrate what their natural talents are at a very early age. One child will be super-focused on building a tall, block structure while another little one is organizing all of the other children to pretend that they are running a store. In contrast to natural gifts, spiritual gifts are abilities you receive when you accept Christ. They are given by the Holy Spirit and are for the glory of God.

What are you naturally good at doing? Do you even know or remember? Never mind whether your family or society thinks it's a big deal or not – you need to see yourself as God's big deal. It is important to review your natural talents so that you can accept them as part and parcel of the amazing person whom you are. Self-acceptance is the first GIFT to give yourself because we are most often manipulated and compromised in the weakest part of our being. If we do not accept who we are we are susceptible to chasing after other people's validation and acceptance of us which is a slippery slope at best and a cruel prison at worst. Make a list of what seems so natural to you that you hardly even consider it a talent. If you get stuck ask anyone who knows you well. Sometimes we get so used to ourselves and our natural gifts that *we* take them for granted!

Become aware of what you are not accepting about yourself. This may sound strange but as a Kingdom-Coach I work with all kinds of people and you would be amazed at how many of them are in denial about their health and physical condition. I often hear: "When I was in the military I could…" or "There was a time when I could _____." The blanks are filled in with some great physical feat of yesterday that has nothing to do with *the present* condition of my clients. It's okay to be proud of what you could do five, ten or even twenty years ago but the truth is you are here now and accepting whatever your "here-now" consists of is one of the biggest steps you must take toward your journey back to wholeness, balance and truth.

Go get the truth you have abandoned, or shoved in the closet, and embrace it with loving arms. I am *this* age; *this* weight; *this* amount of education; *this* net worth; *this* career or job; *this* family; *this* residence; *this* set of accomplishments; and I have *this* dream yet to be realized.

Open your mouth and declare from your heart: I accept myself.

#2 – The GIFT of FORGIVENESS

Hopefully you began un-wrapping the **10 GIFTS** with **The Gift of Self-Acceptance** first. Why? Because it is going to be a much easier task for you to give yourself **The GIFT of Forgiveness** if you *first* accepted yourself. Either way, let's take a look at what is inside of this amazing gift package!

I was raised as a Christian and so I understand the importance of forgiveness in my faith-walk. Since my own sins have been forgiven by the shed blood of Jesus, how dare I not forgive others. Got it. What has taken me longer to get was that I needed to forgive *myself* as well. Wow.

I'd like to share a true story with you; a true story from my own life. Somewhere between my sophomore and junior years at the University of Michigan I decided that I wanted to be a medical doctor; either a neurologist or a cardiologist. Fine. I went to see my counselor and informed him of my decision and signed up for a summer chemistry class. Funny thing about summer classes: they are usually accelerated because the summer semester is shorter than the fall and winter semesters. Chemistry, therefore, is probably not a class I should have taken in the summer. Well I registered and showed up for class fairly confident that I would do well. I had gotten A's in every science class I had ever taken in high school and I was very strong in math. And then a strange thing happened. By the end of the first week the professor had covered just about everything I had learned in high school chemistry. Uh-oh... this was not good. I began struggling to keep up. To cut to the chase, I passed the class with a weak "C" and immediately began to question the wisdom of waiting so late to declare a pre-med major. It went downhill from there.

I took a botany-zoology class, studied like a champion and memorized all kinds of interesting facts and formulas. I was ready for the first exam... or so I thought. The first exam, which proved to be my last one, nearly killed me. To this day I recall with horror, an exam question that began: "If a whale eats a man..." I stared at the exam and question after question was equally foreign to me. Fast forward to me making a beeline to the university office that handled Drop/Add requests. I dropped the class and gave up any more hopes of going to medical school... sorta. I then began a weird, self-defeating dialogue *about* myself *to* myself over my failure to pursue the pre-med curriculum. Years later I was still beating myself up over my failure and then one day, while in prayer, I heard the Lord clearly tell me "Go to medical school or don't go but stop beating yourself up over the fact that you didn't go." In that moment I ***forgave*** myself for not being a medical doctor. I forgave myself for not "trying harder." I forgave myself for "giving up" in botany-zoology. I felt incredibly free from the self-imposed un-forgiveness I had carried around for years and years!

Generally speaking, un-forgiveness locks ***you*** into a prison while the person you won't forgive is free. Forgiving someone else frees you up! But what happens when the person who won't forgive and the person who needs forgiveness are the same person??? (That was me!) Actually, the process and outcome are the same. You get freed-up when you forgive yourself!

What's on your list of things you haven't forgiven yourself for? They're there… draining you of energy, hope and sometimes even the courage to dare something different and fulfilling! Make your list, never mind how short or long it winds up being.

Have you forgiven yourself for not liking your job or career choice? I once had a client who wept bitterly because her family has pressured her into going to law school. They were so proud of her: an Attorney! She hated it. And at the same time she was ashamed of hating what her parents and entire extended family (& friends) were so proud of! Do I even need to mention the guilt she felt over the financial burden to her parents as well as the academic debt she had racked up? After the tears and the shame and the guilt... the bottom line was that she had to forgive herself for her inability to tell her parents, and herself, the truth: she never wanted to go to law school; she hated law school; she hated practicing law. She eventually was able to forgive herself and her parents and the well-meaning community who tried to hang the weight of "Be a Credit to Your Race" around her neck!

Forgive yourself for not having lost 30lbs before the class reunion. Forgive yourself for not having won the Mini-Grant or Genius Award or the Salesperson of the Quarter promotion. Forgive yourself for not being the perfect parent or model spouse or super-saint! Stop apologizing for being a human being with human limitations. Forgive yourself for demanding the absolutely unreasonable things you cooked up for yourself. Ssshhh...

hear that? That's the sound of forgiveness enveloping you with whispers of "you're free now…"

#3 – The GIFT of HEALING

It's time to open up **The Gift of Healing** and not only present it to yourself but apply it to every part of your being that is hurting, wounded, broken, dis-eased or otherwise afflicted. Healing is an interesting word that means different things to different people. What does it mean to you? Does your mind go immediately to physical healing? For many people that is the case, but what about your soul? What about your heart? Can wounded-ness occur in different parts of us? Of course. Then that must mean that different parts of us can experience healing. Absolutely. This gift is going to change your life... watch!

Healing is an adjective that means *becoming sound, well or healthy again; something that heals; curative, remedial, etc.* After reading that I felt compelled to share the root of the word *heal*.

> Heal – to make sound, well, or healthy again; restore to health: as, heal the sick. 2. To cure or get rid of (a disease); restore (a wound, sore, etc.) to healthy

condition. 3. To free from grief, troubles, evil, etc. 4. A) to remedy or get rid of (grief, troubles, etc.). b) to make up (a breach, differences, etc.); reconcile.

Before I talk about healing as a gift you must give yourself, let's first identify some specific areas where healing may be needed in your life.

- **Your BODY:** You may be dealing with some type of illness, condition, malady, or imbalance in your physical body. We are so exquisitely hand-crafted by God that I am perpetually amazed! We are intricately comprised of inter-connected and inter-dependent systems. We have a skeletal system with amazing bones that work together and prevent us from being a heap of parts on the floor. We also have an endocrine system, muscular system, nervous system, circulatory system, digestive system, respiratory system, urinary system and reproductive system. We have over 700 muscles, 206 bones and countless cells and tissues. We are God's masterpiece and physical healing *agrees* with His will for us.
- **Your SOUL:** Your soul has three parts: MIND, WILL and EMOTIONS. If you've ever been deeply grieved or heart-broken then you can recall how your emotions were in a dismal place that crowded out joy, optimism and hope. If you've ever experienced betrayal or

disappointment you know how quickly you lose the "will" to do even ordinary, day-to-day activities. It's easy to lose the will-power to stay with a healthy eating plan if something really disturbing happens to you or those you love. If you have lost the ability to focus your mind on a task due to bad news or an unexpected attack from someone (bullying, verbal abuse, etc.) you know first-hand that you can wrestle with unhealthy thoughts of revenge, self-pity, low self-worth, and other mental states that drain you emotionally.

- **Your SPIRIT:** You are a spirit (who has a soul that lives in a body). God exists in Spirit-form and we too are spirit. As a Christian I believe that each person is born with a "fallen spirit" due to rebellion on the part of Adam and his wife in the Garden. I also believe that when each person accepts Jesus Christ as personal Lord and Savior they receive a *new* spirit:

Therefore if any man be *in Christ,* he is *a new creature: old things are passed away; behold, all things are become new.* 2 Corinthians 5:17 *(KJV)*

These three components, spirit + soul + body, constitute each person. Each of these three can be wounded and each can experience healing which is why **The Gift of Healing** is important for us to explore. Because the root of spiritual healing, for me, is based in my faith, we will look at how to heal wounds to your mind, will and emotions.

Open up **The Gift of Healing** for your SOUL *before* you address dis-ease, dis-comfort and other ailments in your body. Why? Because so many of our energy-leaks, stress-related illnesses, bodily aches and pains are tied directly to what's going on in our soul. Remember – your soul is made up of your mind, will and emotions. Let's look at some specific ways that problems un-attended to in your soul realm result in all kinds of problems that manifest in your body.

The following are five un-healthy habits and problems that add to our stress followed by prescriptive ideas and solutions called Healing Rx:

I. Monster Multi-Tasking – the cultural 'norm' of doing several things at the same time that grows into an uncontrollable monster. When you no longer enjoy pockets of quiet time; when you find yourself unable to focus on only one task without your mind wandering; when you berate yourself for not doing more while you are already doing much – you have probably fallen victim to multi-tasking that is out of control and often leaves you anxious and mentally scattered.

Healing Rx *for* **Monster-Multi-Tasking:**

Experiment for one week by doing ONE THING AT A TIME *only!* Having a meal with a friend or family member? Stay off of your cell phone! Do not, I repeat, do not make airline reservations while waiting for the waiter to serve the main course! Playing with your children? Do not sneak in cleaning out the refrigerator and changing the oil in your car at the same time. If your concern is that you will get *less* done the truth is you will get *more* of what you are supposed to be doing done. Others can tell when we don't give them our full attention. Don't you resent it when you're sharing something meaningful with a friend or spouse and they begin to say "uh-huh" to everything you say? You know that they are not listening and it's insulting. I'd rather someone let my call go into their voicemail than to take my call while ordering food at a drive-thru; pumping gas; watching the game, etc. Do less but pay more attention while you're in engaged.

II. Toxic Time-Traveling – spending way too much time, thought, and emotional energy in your *past* or in your *future* which almost always comes at the expense of the present moment. A sure way to miss the enjoyment of your present life is to never actually be present in it. According to my calendar, today is… today. Our culture is invariably somewhere other than in the day called today. When it's winter we long for spring. When spring ushers in milder temperatures we start pining for summer vacation. When summer temperatures stay in the 80s or 90s we bemoan our burnt lawns. When autumn gifts us with cooler mornings and warm mid-days we whine about the leaves. Hmmmm…. It's not just the weather either. We are always wanting to be older until we actually are and then we wish we had enjoyed being younger.

Healing Rx *for* **Toxic Time-Traveling:**

Here's the cure: Be in today, today. Experience this moment, right now. Consciously choose the healing experience of gratitude for whatever measure of health, wealth, love, material goods, friends, etc. that you presently enjoy. Knock it off with exaggerating about the good ole days – they were alright. Stop fantasizing about how great things will be way up ahead in the future – there's no guarantee that those you intend to share it with will even be alive. Of course you can, and should, set goals, pursue dreams, etc. but not so much that you totally miss out on the splendor and simplicity of this present moment.

Breathe in and say: *"I am alive..."* Breathe out and say: *"... in this very moment."* Breathe in and say: *"When this moment passes..."* Breathe out and say: *"...I will never see it again."*

III. Options-Overload – having way too many options actually slows down your decision-making process while increasing your stress levels. Have you noticed that it is becoming more and more difficult to go to the market and purchase a basic item like a loaf of bread or jar of mustard? It seems like every product has at least 50 variations from which to choose. Want a loaf of bread? No problem. Let's see... you can have wheat or honey wheat or enriched, low calorie, no salt wheat, etc. Same is true of mustard. Did you want honey-Dijon or pimento relish mustard with capers and jalapenos? Too many choices actually lead to stress.

Healing Rx *for* **Options-Overload**

I hereby recommend the following prescription: as much as you are able, know in advance what you'd like to purchase and frequent the same stores whose layout is familiar. It can save time and lower your stress level if you are able to get in and out of a place because you know where to find the items you've come to purchase. In addition to that, do not be shy about asking store personnel for help when you aren't familiar with a store.

Overloaded by clothing options? Go through your closet and get honest about what you love; what you know looks good on you and what fits you properly. Remove clothes that are not seasonal or that do not fit the three criteria just given. Less really is more. Color-code your weekday clothes for faster mix & match. If you are experiencing a particular busy or demanding season of your life (illness, work or family demands, grief, etc.) photograph outfits that work so that you don't have to think about 'putting them together' each morning. You could also try laying out your wardrobe the week before or night before to save yourself some energy. A relatively small amount of pre-planning meals, shopping, clothes selections and even routine house-cleaning might reduce the strain on you significantly. Select - simplify!

IV. Destructive-Distractions – addiction to tiny, up-to-the-second units of miscellaneous, irrelevant data in the forms of social media posts, tweets, texts, pictures, and TV surfing that involves literally hundreds of options at any given moment via countless devices. Our fear of 'missing out on something' has caused us to slavishly stay connected when our souls yearn for rest.

Healing Rx *for* **Destructive Distractions**

Decide what is important to you: in your life and in the moment. Learn to prioritize what is most important and learn to focus on specific tasks, conversations, and thoughts without drifting all over the place. Mute phones during dinner or yoga class. Resist the urge to check posts while in the movies. Select specific times of the day to return emails, update posts, respond to friends, and so on. Practice watching one program at a time on TV without surfing channels during commercials. Practice ignoring smart phones during dinner time or social events (funerals, weddings, surgeries, etc.). Take periodic breaks from your virtual world to be fully present in the actual world. Reduce clutter. Organize home and work spaces so that when you need a particular item whether clothing, a document or a tool, you can easily locate it and not get distracted by all of the other things you have to wade through in your search. Prioritize – organize – focus!

V. Chronic-Comparisons – The self-defeating habit of always comparing what you have, do for a living, house you live in, salary you earn, education you've acquired, children and spouse's accomplishment will wear you out. There are entire, multi-million dollar industries that thrive on your dissatisfaction with your life when compared to some ideal that is often manufactured and unrealistic!

Others get rich by banking on the fact that you will compare yourself to some ideal and, when you fall short, buy their product. Sound familiar? Whiter teeth. Shinier hair. Flatter abs. Longer lashes. Less wrinkles. Greater endurance. Less fat – *always* less fat!!! Let's not leave out what to wear! I am not opposed to Fashion Week in New York or Paris but when you buy into the notion that *unless* you perpetually step out "GQ" or look like the Princess, First Lady or the plethora of runway models and photo-shopped cover-girls something is amiss. When you overspend only to discover the outfit looks different on you then it did on the runway; when you experience mild depression because of someone else's good fortune or PR-generated 'image' you aren't appreciating your own grand gift of life. I could say more but you get the picture. There will always be someone richer, younger, taller, smarter, or better connected than you BUT there will never be someone BETTER at BEING YOU than YOU.

Healing Rx *for* **Chronic-Comparisons**

The cure for chronically comparing yourself to others (or even yourself when you were younger, thinner, healthier, etc.) can be summed up in one powerful word: ***gratitude***. I remember years ago when Oprah encouraged her audience to keep gratitude journals. I have friends who, to this day, continue to record what they are grateful for on a daily basis. If the thought of keeping a journal sounds like too much work for you, that's okay. Perhaps the simple practice of ending each day as well as beginning each day with a prayer of gratitude may help you re-center your heart on *what really matters* and raise your awareness of how incredibly blessed you already are.

If I challenged you, this very moment, to stop reading this book and close your eyes while recounting all of the things, people, opportunities, resources, experiences, and joys that you are genuinely, deeply grateful for… well it just might surprise you how long your list is. Don't want a gratitude journal? How about a gratitude whiteboard? Try a mason jar, coffee can or beautiful basket into which you could place slips of paper that you've written gratitude acknowledgements upon. This is doable. It is powerful and it is contagious. The next time someone asks "How are you today?" say: "Grateful!"

Healing is all about restoring the optimum state and divine equilibrium of life. Your heart beats non-stop your entire life but, in between beats, it rests. All animals rest and some even hibernate. As a matter of fact, some trees and plants go into a season of resting from producing leaves and fruit. So much of our illness stems from minds that we have forgotten how to quiet and hearts that resist peace.

Healing is about receiving. It is time, or perhaps even past due time, for you to re-learn the art and beauty of allowing healing to occur in your body and your soul. Make time for healing. Expect it and welcome it when it manifests.

#4 – The GIFT of SELF-DISCOVERY

"You cannot nurture yourself unless, and until, you understand your nature!"

Before this book was a book, it was a workshop and then a seminar and then a standing-room only celebration of the journey back to self. When I first began conducting **10 GIFTS** as a workshop I found this amazing set of nesting boxes (which are on the cover). To me they were the *perfect symbol* for self-discovery because each box has a lid and each box fits into another box. Similarly, when we commit to the life-long process of *dis*-covering what God has so lovingly placed within us, we will find more and more treasures as we go deeper and deeper in Him. It is in the process of *dis*-covering those internal gift boxes (removing the covers) that we are able to view what is inside.

Take a moment right now to imagine your life as a set of nesting boxes, each with a lid. What will you find when you start removing lids? What do your treasure boxes contain? That, my dear friend, is the quest before you as you give yourself the amazing **Gift of Self-Discovery**!

You have Permission to Look Inside…

Before we begin I just want to share one more point for you to ponder: when we do *not* give ourselves ***permission*** to look inside of ourselves we usually wind up accepting *what others tell* us is inside.

If you loved music or art as a young child and a well-meaning parent (family member or teacher) discouraged you by saying "You'll never make a living as an artist or musician" then not only did they fail to *really see* what was in your box, but they may have also de-valued something in your essence. They may have influenced you to pursue something other than what God ordained. Since most of us love and trust our parents, we thought that they *knew best* and we sometimes pushed the art or music deep down underneath some things in our heart; *beneath what they said* was best for us.

Although it lay dormant, the good news is that it never really went away! If God placed it in your heart, beloved, it's *never* going away! Now… let's look inside…

Here are **three** ways to exhume your own buried treasures: (1) Solo Self-Discovery, (2) Group Self-

Discovery, and (3) Guided Self-Discovery. Pick whichever method, or combination of methods, will work best for you:

➢ *Solo* Self-Discovery

For **Phase One** of your **"Solo" Self-Discovery** process you will need a few supplies: a pen; journal or notebook; 3-ring binder; large poster board; glue-stick or tape; and scissors.

JOURNAL – In your journal or notebook write your responses to the following questions. Take your time and ***do not*** edit, judge, criticize or critique your answers. Simply let your innermost heart answer each question without your paradigms interrupting or interfering:

- You have just inherited $ 100,000 tax-free. What would you do with it?
- You have just received a $1,000,000 (Yes, one million dollars) Genius Grant to use anyway you'd like to advance your own creativity, passions, inner-calling, or life-long dream. What would you do with it? (Be detailed)
- You have exactly one year to live. Money is no object. How would you spend your last year of life?

Be sure to include the date of when you respond because if you repeat this activity at another time in the year or in later years you often will discover that your answers to the questions change.

3-RING BINDER – Similar to the instructions for the journal and the image board, the goal is to collect images, words, symbols and phrases that symbolically explain what your heart is speaking to you. The advantage of a 3-ring binder is that you can create tabbed-divided sections for different parts of your life, for example, a section on career, another section on recreation and still another for relationships. There is no right or wrong way to do this and there is no reason for you to be restricted in how you go about it… so… set your binder up anyway you please and enjoy!

POSTER BOARD – On a large poster board (or two) create a collage of images, words, phrases, etc. that depict what your "ideal" life looks like. In order to complete this Self-Discovery project you will need a variety of magazines so I recommend that you first treat yourself to a small shopping spree at a bookstore or Flea Market that sells a large variety of publications. Intentionally buy magazines that you would not necessarily read: travel, fitness, psychology, golfing, business, and so on. The reason is that you will open yourself up to pictures, words and advertisements that are 'outside of the box' for you and you may be pleasantly surprised to find images that resonate with something *you did not know* was in your heart.

For all three of the **Self-Discovery** projects you are always welcome to write down words, phrases or Scriptures and add them to your display.

The ***Phase Two*** part of this process is for you to give yourself time to reflect on what you created in the journal, 3-ring binder or image board. What patterns do you notice? What, if any, are recurrent themes? Did your assignment 'touch' anything you dreamed about *when you were a child?* Have you lived out any of the things you desire and if so, to what extent? This part of self-discovery cannot be rushed. Please sit quietly with what you find. Honor it by allowing it to be present with you – like a long-lost friend who has finally come to visit. Be. Still. Listen. Honor.

Finally, for your ***Phase Three*** task, decide what action you will take to rearrange your life to incorporate more of what you want into your life! YOU are the architect of your life. YOU are the conductor of your own orchestra. YOU wield the brushes upon the God-given canvas called "your life." This is by far your most HONEST moment; the moment you decide to embrace and pursue what you know is in your heart.

➤ *Group* Self-Discovery

If you prefer to be a part of the wonderful energy, and synergy, of a group who is comprised of like-minded, determined, and focused individuals then the **"Group" Self-Discovery** process is an excellent choice. The **"Group" Self-Discovery** experience consists of your participation in a community of like-minded souls. Through a Webinar format you open boxes with others and benefit from group interaction & shared exploration. You also get direct access to me – as your Facilitator & Coach. The advantages of this method include the convenience of interactive participation plus the opportunity to review the recorded webinar sessions at your leisure. You also benefit from the questions and challenges of others because often an answer given to another may be just the idea that transforms your own journey experience.

In an invigorating, compassionate virtual community you will enjoy the opportunity to hear other's questions, comments, and inspiring examples of progress in self-discovery. As a member of the **10 GIFTS Community** you will also gain access to additional resources and information to facilitate your personal growth & development. *(Please visit the Sterling-Xavier website for more information on registration and dates of events.)*

➢ ***Guided*** *Self-Discovery*

Yet another self-discovery support option for you is that of the one-on-one, customized, **10 GIFTS-Coaching**. As a Life Coach I will work directly with you to ensure that the goals, activities, practices and reflections that you set for yourself actually yield fruit. If you find areas that are challenging, I will show you alternate ways of approaching the situation and of making headway in, through or around them. The **10 GIFTS-Coaching** experience will allow you to focus *exclusively* on what *your* needs are.

Whichever method, or combination of methods, you choose, your decision to give yourself **The Gift of Self-Discovery** is by far one of the most life affirming gifts you'll receive. The reason is that no two individuals are identical. Your particular temperament, learning style, communications style, background, educational and experience profile is... well... unique just like your fingerprint is unique. It is not until you understand who you really are that you can live a full and maximized life.

I always knew that honoring all parts of my essence was the goal but, it wasn't until I accepted my unique desire to blend passions of scholarship, entrepreneurship, artistry and ministerial service that I no longer felt like a misfit. The truth is that I'm not a misfit and neither are you. We all have gifts and abilities that must be honored and nurtured. Let the **Gift of Self-Discovery** be the guide to understanding your purpose as well as the foundation that supports future life choices and decision-making.

#5 – The GIFT of SELF-AFFIRMATION

"Words are like seeds; when planted they develop roots, grow and produce fruit."

Most likely you are already familiar with the term 'affirmation' and understand it to be a statement, saying or phrase that builds up and encourages as opposed to tearing down and negating. According to Random House Webster College Dictionary, affirmation means:

> "1. the act of affirming state of being affirmed; 2. the assertion that something exists or is true; 3. something that is affirmed or declared to be true; 4. confirmation or ratification of a prior judgment decision etc; 5. a solemn declaration accepted instead of a statement under oath" (Source: http://www.definitions/Random)

When you participate in the act of affirming your *own* state of being, and when you assert that something in or about you is true, you wield tremendous, transformative, healing and life-giving power over your own life!

Open **The Gift of Self-Affirmation** this very moment and begin, or enhance, the process of *speaking* life into your life. You literally contain miracles in your mouth. In the Bible we find the origin of all that exists as Elohim (Elohim means 'God' in the plural form of the word) speaks life into existence (Genesis 1:1). *All* words have power because *all* words are like seed that reproduce. If you are called stupid or ugly often enough by someone you respect and trust, those harsh words will take root in your self-perception and invariably, unless rooted out, sprout seedlings of doubt, low self-esteem and self-loathing. These seedlings eventually produce fruit of self-doubt, self-sabotage, and sometimes toleration for abuse. Likewise, if someone you know and trust speaks words that convey you are smart, creative, beautiful, a joy to be around, and wonderful, eventually those words will take root and produce fruit of a life gilded with self-acceptance, self-confidence, smart decisions, healthy boundaries, and self-appreciation.

Regardless of whom you may have listened to in your past, by opening **The Gift of Self-Affirmation**, you can begin immediately to plant *new seeds* of self-esteem and self-acceptance. Here are four ways to experience self-affirmation:

1. Collect positive statements. Personalize positive statements by inserting your name into the phrase and then speaking the statements out loud on a regular basis. I've actually created a number of Affirmation Cards that compile statements you can tailor to build up your reserve of positive self-thoughts. One very popular product is *"I Am a Woman of Virtue"* that uses Scriptures paraphrased into affirming statements. These, as well as affirmational recordings are available at my website but let's talk about how you can create your own line.

2. Make a list of desirable attributes. Make a list of desired attributes, such as: "I am a confident salesperson" or "I am a successful speaker." As you might imagine when you speak your customized, tailored-made list of affirmations on a regular basis it serves to re-shape your thinking, refill your emotional fuel tank, and strengthen your overall self-image. Just remember – the transformative power of self-affirmations is activated by *speaking* them out loud often.

3. Place affirming statements throughout your environment. While lists of affirmations are wonderful, powerful, and truly will make a difference when spoken out loud on a regular basis, another brilliant way to engage in the practice of self-affirmation is to include affirming statements as artwork throughout your work and home environments. You can easily print a statement and frame it to be hung in your bedroom or bathroom so that the first things you see each morning is a greeting of positive energy. Depending upon the type of work environment you have, you might be able to hang or place a framed statement on your desk. Bookmarks, wallet cards and small magnets are also great specialty gifts to give you micro-bursts of self-affirmation throughout the day. Remember the Image Board you learned about in Chapter 5 – **The Gift of Self-Discovery**? Well there is no reason why you can't create an Image Board full of self-affirming statements.

    4. Build a library of audio affirmations. If you have time available during the commute to school or work; quiet time early in the morning or late in the evening; a break time during the day; or other opportunities to listen to a CD or MP3 recording, consider listening to affirmations from your own audio library. I have a companion CD for this book: "*10 Gifts to Give Yourself – Affirmations*" but I also recommend the powerful recordings available from people such as Joyce Meyers, Dr. Creflo Dollar and Joel Osteen. There are many motivational and inspirational speakers, teachers, coaches and ministers whose messages may resonate with you in a special way. Listening to positive and affirming messages will reinforce the statements (and images) you have placed throughout your environment and spoken over your life. Words that begin as seeds will eventually create gardens of fruit-bearing beliefs, expectations and actions.

#6 – The GIFT of SELF-DEVELOPMENT

The Gift of Self-Development is going to require that you make a serious commitment to invest in yourself. While in the previous chapter we talked about the power of the positive statements you repeatedly speak to yourself, **The Gift of Self-Development** is going to challenge you to move beyond *speaking* into 'building' your life. What do I mean by 'building' your life? I mean that you will need to explore what it will require, in terms of training, education, experience, interning, practice, mentoring and so forth, for you to reach your goals.

Years ago I knew that I wanted to build a business as an Educational Consultant but I had a problem. In spite of the fact of having obtained a B.A. degree in psychology, I hadn't taken any educational classes in undergrad nor had I pursued a K-12 teaching certificate. What I *had* done was study a lot of educational and cognitive psychology on my own. Hmmm… what to do? I decided to return to school and obtain a Master's Degree in Education. This degree gave me the credibility to stand before teachers, administrators, counselors and parents and legitimately address the cognitive issues their students were having. In my particular case I continued my education and obtained doctoral degrees in education, philosophy and eventually in theology. Each degree was an investment in my life that supported my goals!

Before you open **The Gift of Self-Development** you need to have done some in-depth work on **Self-Discovery** because you don't want to waste your time developing something that you aren't in love with! And... for the record, **Self-Development** doesn't automatically mean a college degree. It may mean volunteering with an organization to learn its inner-workings. It might involve becoming a Sous Chef if your dream is to one day be Head Chef. It may mean pursuing accreditation as a Yoga Instructor if your goal is to open your own studio. It could also mean taking an informal path. By informal I am referring to a non-structured, non-credentialing experience. You may need to serve as an unpaid intern to get some experience needed that has nothing to do with a formal degree, certificate, accreditation or license.

As you open **The Gift of Self-Development** resist the urge to talk yourself out of what you need by saying you don't have the time or money. When you are really ready to invest in yourself you will find a way to make it happen and others will help you. The investment you make in yourself promises to yield a 'return on investment' that cannot be measured in dollars and cents exclusively but also in personal fulfillment, spiritual meaning and personal joy as you live a life of purpose. Here are five steps to open and enjoy this gift:

STEP 1: **Begin by clearly stating what you want.** So what it is, exactly, that you want? Your answer to this question is the most important part of benefiting from the **Gift of Self-Development**. Do you want something that will enhance you physically or health-wise? Do you desire to master a new skill? Do you want a license, credential, academic or vocational certification, or college degree? Do you want to know more about finances? Take your time and don't just *think* about your answer, but *commit your answer to writing*.

STEP 2: **State what you need to do.** What you need to 'do' may be a combination of formal and informal things so be as specific as possible when stating what you need to do *before* you begin researching the process.

STEP 3: **Conduct research**. In order to get what you want you may need to research aspects of the process: resources, opportunities, grants, schooling, internships, support, technology, or materials. So do your 'research' homework because the better informed you are the easier it will be to create an exciting and practical plan.

STEP 4: **Draft a plan for your self-development**. Put it in writing. Your plan will state your *goal* (what you want); a *rationale* (why you want it); *resources* required (who / what is needed); *a timeline* (when you want it); a *budget* (how much it will cost); and specific steps you can take to make it happen (how it will be accomplished). In business there is a common statement: "A goal without a deadline is a wish." In drafting your self-development plan don't forget to include dates and deadlines even if they have to be altered as you go along.

STEP 5: **Begin carrying out your plan**. Take the first step! Then take the next step, and the next one, and don't stop stepping until you have accomplished your self-development goals.

STEP 6: **Get an accountability partner**. This is optional but highly recommended. If you struggle with discouragement and false-starts, let someone you trust know you need their help in holding you accountable for making progress.

STEP 7: **Get a prayer partner**. This too is optional and highly recommended. In addition to my spouse, I have two prayer partners. I pray with each of them (separately) on different days of the week. We've been praying for over five years and I'm sure that their prayers have helped me pursue my God-given dreams in ways that I can't measure.

STEP 8: **Celebrate!** Be sure to celebrate the achievement of your self-development goals. I threw a party when I received my Master's Degree and another one when I got my first PhD. I had a Book Signing Party when I published my first book. When you've work diligently on a goal make sure that celebrating your accomplishments is a part of the plan as well.

#7 – The GIFT of CONSCIOUS CHOOSING

According to many behavioral psychologists it takes 21 days to *form a habit*. Whether you are aware of it or not there are many actions you take and thoughts you have that occur without *conscious thinking* because they have become habits. Most likely you sit in the same place at Church; park in the same spot at work; brush your teeth with the same hand each morning; and shop at the same grocery store.

Our habits are not necessarily good or bad. In most instances they are beneficial because they save us time by freeing up the mental energy we would otherwise use if we had to stop and think about every behavior every time. I mean really – do you have any idea how draining it would be to have to decide which way to drive home or which drawer you will place your clean t-shirts in? If you did this it would probably create chaos and you might not ever find your t-shirts!

If you leave your keys in the same place each day, not only do I not want to tamper with that habit, I actually want to encourage you to continue – finding your keys is a good thing (smile).

But what happens when *too much* of your day-to-day living becomes an enormous blob of robot-like habits??? Yikes! The exact same routine: same breakfast, same driving route, same coffee shop, same TV programs at night with the same snack (a bowl of popcorn or pint of ice cream). A life somehow set on autopilot… **STOP!** You need **The Gift of Conscious Choosing**.

Quick-scan your wardrobe. Is that red and white, hand-knitted, woolen scarf around your neck there because you love it or because you don't want to hurt the feelings of the well-meaning, but style-challenged relative who gave it to you three years ago? What would *you* like to wear? What would make you feel fabulous while also accomplishing the very real function of keeping you warm?

Today, as you are reading these words, a revolution has just begun! From now on you will engage in what I like to call *random acts of conscious-choosing quick scans*! You will pay attention to what you are doing and thinking and then immediately quick-scan the action or thought to find out if you have consciously chosen it or if it a dusty, outdated, no longer relevant, tired, routine, thoughtless choice.

I recall being invited to a wonderful social event with great people in an amazing venue. Problem was… I did not want to attend. I was delightfully knee-deep in writing this book and it was cold outside and I didn't know anyone who would be there except the couple who thought I might enjoy attending. I didn't want to hurt this couple's feelings and I realize that they really don't know how much of an introvert I am or that sitting at home writing feels like a little slice of heaven to me…blah, blah, blah. I *nearly* accepted the invitation but alas, I came to my senses and consciously choose to pass on the invitation! I felt exhausted trying to imagine myself going but felt immediate relief when I stood in my truth and admitted that I did not want to go and that I would not go. Think it's simple? We'll see…

How do you open **The Gift of Conscious Choosing** for yourself? You begin by understanding and accepting that your choices are absolutely going to bother, irritate, confuse or annoy others who want you to choose what *they want* you to choose! Got that? Are you sure? Sit with that reality for a few minutes so that you can be prepared when others launch entire campaigns to get you to change your mind.

Let's begin with something small so that you can build capacity. How about food? Chances are you eat every day and chances are you are eating foods, sometimes, that others think you should eat. Pay attention in the next week or so, especially in social settings, to the choices you make. At the corporate gala when someone insists you try some of the goose pate and you don't want to. JUST SAY NO... well, say "no thanks." When they keep saying, "try it, try it!" ignore them and reach for the salmon crostini with a touch of cream cheese and capers. **Consciously choose** what you wear; where you sit; how long you stay in social media; where you go for lunch and how much you consume when you get there.

After you've had enough practice with **consciously choosing** relatively small thoughts and actions advance to the next levels: relationships and career (but not in the same day). Review your closest relationships which will most likely be significant others, family and roommate or housemate. After that circle of people the next closest group will probably involve those with whom you work or go to school. Repeating the process stated earlier, spend one week simply *paying attention* to interactions with others. Do you manipulate others? Are you manipulated? Do others whine to get their way (do you)? Is there someone in your life who gets their way by threatening to leave you or do they withhold affection, conversation or attention? Do you do any of these? Stop. Stand in your truth. Be honest and then make a **conscious choice** to neither manipulate others nor be manipulated by them!

If you read chapter 6, **The Gift of Self-Affirmation**, by now you should have a healthy amount of positive and affirming statements that you make about yourself to help counter the threats of others withdrawing their energy from you. If this requires more support than you had imagined please do not hesitate to seek spiritual, psychological or other kinds of therapeutic assistance. Habits formed years ago and reinforced for years and years are no longer simply habits but have become a lifestyle. In spiritual terms we call negative habits 'strongholds' that can be broken through faith, prayer and the Word of God.

An amazing benefit of **conscious choosing** is that it requires you to get to know yourself better *and* to honor yourself. I have actually caught myself saying "I really do not want to have this conversation if it involves putting someone else down." The person with whom I was speaking was at first startled and then replied "You sure don't like talking about people do you?" Well... no I don't. It's mean-spirited and un-Christ like. There are literally billions of topics for us to choose from so, no, I don't want to make fun of another person. Quick-scan your thoughts, conversations, behaviors, and feelings; are they choices or habits?

The Gift of Conscious Choosing has the potential to change the quality of your days. You can choose to see the proverbial glass as half empty or half full. You can choose to hold out hope for a fallen world and then let your prayers lift this hope up to heaven as a compassionate and fragrant prayer of intercession for others. You can choose to wear jazzy colors that you enjoy or earth tones because that's what works for you. Choose to eat more fruit and vegetables while staying hydrated; read one good book a month; learn Tai Chi or a new hustle; the sky is the limit for what you can choose. WOW – I love this gift. I hope that you do too. I hope that even the *mere thought* of consciously choosing causes you to look at your life through sparkling new lenses. Choose something different. Choose something better. Choose something - consciously!

#8 – The GIFT of SELF-NURTURING

I have a 'thought experiment' for you before we explore **The Gift of Self-Nurturing**. Let's imagine you were asked to nurture three different living creatures back to health, assuming that each had been neglected and is now weak and sickly. You say 'Yes' and then are given a goldfish, a sheep, and an eagle. All are mature as opposed to being newly born. To make your task easier you receive a magnificent aquarium, a pasture with streams and rivers, and some acreage that includes high, rocky cliffs. You also receive plenty of food that each creature is known to eat. You are told that if you should find that any of your three charges require anything else for restoration, healing and sustenance you have an unlimited credit line at your disposal. Oh… and to make sure that the goldfish, sheep and eagle are faring well, someone will come out to check on them on an unannounced, random basis! You agree. Days go by followed by weeks. Finally, on the third day of the fifth month you look out your window and see an unfamiliar van approaching. As it gets closer you recognize the name and logo of the organization that placed the living creatures in your care months ago.

They get out of the van, introduce themselves and request to see the goldfish, the sheep and the eagle. You have already broken out into a profuse sweat and now your knees are starting to buckle. You trip over your words and start mumbling *"I did the best I could... I did my best... I used everything you all gave me but they all died shortly after I got them... it's not my fault; after all they were weak and sickly when you brought them here... I did my best..."*

Confused, the inspectors ask what exactly you had done. From a place of genuine sorrow you explain: *"I took the sheep up to a high, rocky cliff and left her there. I placed the eagle in the aquarium and covered the lid – I'm positive the temperature of the water was alright. Oh... I placed the goldfish out in the pasture not more than 3 or 4 feet from the stream in case it got thirsty."*

Let's stop here. A child in elementary school would be able to tell you what you did wrong. You did not **nurture** *according to* the **nature** of each creature. While you may have cared deeply (since the transcript states you were genuinely sorry for their deaths) the bottom line is it didn't matter how wonderful each setting was if it was not according to the nature of the particular creature. The fish could not survive in the grassy pasture near the water. The eagle, as majestic and awesome as it is, had no chance once it was submerged underwater in the confines of the aquarium, and the sheep most likely starved to death or was mortally wounded by predators without the watchful eye of a shepherd and access to grass and peaceful water.

Now, open **The Gift of Self-Nurturing** with the heightened awareness that regardless of how wonderful someone else's "setting" is, *you* must be ***nurtured*** according to *your **nature*** or else you will get weaker and weaker until the joy of life is completely gone.

Your first work, in order to enjoy this particular gift, is to fully understand your nature. Yes, yes we both know that you are a human being and therefore require air, food, rest, etc. That's not the nature I am referring to. I mean the nature of *you* that is completely unique to you. What causes *you* to thrive! What makes *your* eyes light up with delight or *your* heart burst into song? Be patient with this self-examination because it is critical to your healing and restoration. You won't make it back to yourself unless you acknowledge what your nature is and how it is your life's responsibility, as a steward of your own self, to nurture you.

Let me share a personal example. As a very young child, age of 4, I experienced an unusual sensitivity to Crayola Crayons. Yep. I felt sheer delight when I opened the box of 8 colors. One day my father gave me and my older sister, money to buy whatever we wanted. She and I headed straight to the closest neighborhood store and made our selections quickly. She bought candy and you *know* what I bought… a box of Crayola Crayons!!! I still recall my parent's surprise over my selection. Don't get me wrong, I liked candy but I *loved* crayons.

Go deep inside the vault of your heart where true joy resides. What's in there? Is it a box of crayons? Is it the sensation of gliding through water? Is it dance? Is it the smell of clay and the feel of the potter's wheel spinning? Or, is it warmth that floods you when you hear a jazz saxophonist in person? Whatever it is it stirs your passion. Start with passion! What moves you deeply? Finish this sentence and then finish it again and again:

"*I love* _____."

I love jazz. I love tai chi. I love roller-skating. I love the sound of children laughing. I love bookstores. I love encouraging people and giving them hope. I love good preaching. I love the smell of chicken frying and the sounds of my friends in my home laughing and talking with each other. I love museums and art galleries. I love… I love… I love….!

There are many who recommend keeping a gratitude journal. Sounds good to me. But I also recommend an "I LOVE _____" journal because you may be grateful for not having to sleep outdoors but that is a different energy than "I love deep sea diving." Again, "I am grateful a roof over my head" is qualitatively different from "I love volunteering to help people learn to read." One seems more like a passive acknowledgement while the other seems more like a declaration of a specific wellspring of personal JOY.

Start writing that list. Take hours or days to try and capture everything you can think of that truly brings a gi-normous (gigantic + enormous = gi-normous!!!) electrifying, energizing response from within; one that bubbles up from deep inside and finally overflows into a fountain of personal joys.

When you have seriously tried to exhaust a list of what you love and allowed yourself to be immersed in the positive feelings such reflections evoke, then you can review your list and *listen* to it. That's right – LISTEN. Your list of things *you love* is speaking to you and telling you many ways that you need to **nurture** yourself. *Selah**

Keep your list where you can easily review it. On any given day, during any given week – how much self-nurturing do you practice? If you peruse your list it should be easy to determine whether or not you have bothered to feed your inner-soul. Using **The Gift of Conscious Choosing**, choose something from your list and then choose to immerse yourself in it! Like a houseplant whose leaves droop from too little water, your soul can droop. As you practice Self-Nurturing, you'll experience vibrant revitalization. This is not your mate's job or your boss or your friends. This is your job.

The Gift of Self-Nurturing is a healing gift that begins in self-truth. This is your hard work – your sacred assignment.

#9 – The GIFT of SELF-LOVE

Given the other eight GIFTS you've already presented to yourself, opened and enjoyed, how is it that a **Gift of Self-Love** is needed? Glad you asked. This Gift is included because you need to understand what un-conditional love *really* means; you need to challenge yourself to *receive it* from God; give it to *yourself* and then to others – in that order.

Unconditional love. You've heard the phrase before. You understand it, at least at face-value. It means to love without placing conditions on or in front of the love. You may even practice it with others… maybe. I have a son who is now an adult. When he was a baby I understood unconditional love. When he became a toddler – no problem, I still understood it. He went through puberty and entered his teen years… and… I was forced to explore my so-called understanding of unconditional love for him. Because of my faith, my church family and the prayers of the righteous – my definition held firm. I realized, with the gentlest peace, that I really, really loved my son *regardless* of what happened in school that day. I love him beyond his teacher's opinions and beyond how he kept his room. My loving him had nothing to do with his academic performance, trumpet practice, giftedness, or any chores he managed to complete or forget (or ignore). I told him so. Loving him without "conditions" made it easier for me to see his unique temperament, intellectual genius, and wonderful personality! Loving others around me without "condition" has the exact same effect. I am fascinated by different cultures and different ethnicities. I tend to see the beauty in others long before I am aware of their flaws and when I look at others, I see the divine craftsmanship of God in making them who they are.

But what happens when I look in the mirror. Oh Lord! The truth is… I used to see every shortcoming, every failure, every flaw, error and mistake. I saw physical imperfections as well as psychological ones. I berated myself for being shy and introverted. Even into adulthood I belittled myself for not going to medical school. I nagged me for not saving more money; for not building a bigger company and so forth and so on. Then one day, while I was studying grace and God's unconditional love for us, I finally got it. I am loved. I am loved without condition and so are you.

When I pray I often say "I love you back Lord!" and while I was teaching a year-long class called "Out of the Box Bible Study" the Lord told me that I love Him **with conditions**. Um…. What? That is exactly what He said and I heard Him clearly. He asked me if I would love Him more when more of my books sold or if Oprah would call and invite me on her show or if a mega-church ordered 10,000 of my books while inviting me to come and speak? I quietly said 'no'. He then explained that I was to love Him without conditions. I understood. Later I understood that we are to love Him, ourselves, and others without conditions.

So, now, back to you. Tell the truth: Will you love yourself *more* when you finish your degree; lose ten pounds; write a book; go back to school; find a job; get a promotion; buy a bigger house or car or purse? Think about it.

Open **The Gift of Self-Love** and present it to yourself. If you are serious about this – go get a mirror. Look into your own eyes and first apologize for every "condition-based" hurtful comment or thought you've had about the person staring back at you in the mirror. Apologize and mean it. Next – accept your apology and mean it! Forgive yourself for what you said and thought (about yourself) and forgive yourself for hearing it and believing it.

Use **The Gift of Self-Love** to inventory what you embrace about yourself. Start wherever you want but I suggest the physical realm because we are often the most harsh when it comes to our physical appearance and/or body type. If you have a full-length mirror, disrobe and look at your body with acceptance and love. It has served you well all these many years. It's time to appreciate your body and then love how incredible it is.

You should know what's coming next – yes I want you to open your mouth and say *"I love me. I am glad to be alive. I love my heart, lungs, liver, brain and every other hard-working organ in my body."* Don't stop! Speak to whatever you can see or feel and tell yourself how much you love and appreciate your fingers, toes, eyes, ears, skin, knees, etc. End by once again looking in your own eyes and saying, *"I love you (say your name) without condition."* SAY IT AGAIN two more times: *"I love you (say your name) without condition. I love you (say your name) without condition."* Then say: *"I love you as God loves you – without condition. Amen."*

When you love someone you enjoy their company. You enjoy getting to know them and you enjoy doing nice things for them. Hint, hint: all of this should be true for you. Enjoy spending time with yourself. Don't just tolerate yourself – enjoy your time alone. Got a day off or a weekend to yourself? Fix yourself a great breakfast and enjoy a spa-like bath, or get dressed and take yourself to a favorite breakfast place and enjoy reading a book. Do nice things for yourself. There is no need to break the bank either – learn how to do nice things for yourself without incurring debt. Make your own wish list of affordable gifts: a new golf putter, a leather journal, a professional massage, a subscription to a favorite magazine, etc.

Since you are learning to love yourself, keep all medical appointments! Take care of your health. Cut back on refined sugar and flour. Reduce your salt intake. Drink more water and get more sleep! Laugh more and place a permanent moratorium on complaining.

The Gift of Self-Love is in alignment with how God feels about you. Remember, He loves you so much that He sent His only begotten Son to redeem you from sin and grant you eternal life! You are loved *without condition* by **God**. Accept and agree with His love, return it, love yourself and then love others!

#10 – The GIFT of BALANCE

The Gift of Balance is the final gift in this wonderful set of **10 GIFTS**! Open this Gift in order to restore boundaries for yourself and re-learn how to establish spiritual, emotional, relational and psychological **balance** in all areas of your life.

Beloved, our God is a God of excellence. Everything He made is beautiful – including you. When you are out of balance you are in danger of being depleted, unstable and disoriented. Have you ever had your automobile tires 'balanced'? Unbalanced tires will destabilize your car and affect your driving and riding experience. Eventually your tires will wear down in an uneven pattern. Without balance in your life, eventually YOU will wear down in an uneven pattern!

I don't know exactly how you give *too much* of yourself away but from experience as a coach and as a minister I'm fairly certain it stems from an imbalanced view of what you owe other people.

Other people's expectations. Other people have expectations of YOU and your time, energy, resources, money, love, support, anointing, weekends, car, and service! Sound familiar? It should. Somehow in the course of loving others we lose our way. We erase, or allow others to erase, boundaries. We teach others how to treat us! If everybody's agenda is more important than yours it will not take long for you to be out of balance AND to make matters even worse, you have inadvertently *taught them* to diminish or devalue you.

Do you have the energy to unwrap one more **Gift**? Good. Open up **The Gift of Balance** and present yourself with a *Permission Slip to Establish Boundaries* and a *Declaration of Independence from Imbalance*.

Your *Permission Slip to Establish Boundaries* is similar to the permission slip your teacher would pass out in order for you to go on a field trip. It outlined where you were going; the date and time of the outing; specific requirements with regards to lunch plans; spending money needed; and information about the family physician as well as names of emergency contacts. In addition to all of this a parent or legal guardian's signature was required. It wasn't that the teacher, or the school for that matter, didn't trust you; on the contrary. The school wanted to make sure that whoever was caring for you (parents or guardians) knew exactly where you would be once you left school property. The school wanted to make sure you were prepared for the outing; that you had the right fees if you were attending something that required admission or money for a gift shop. They wanted to communicate how you would be fed – whether lunch was included or you needed to bring a bag lunch or money for the cafeteria. The school needed someone, who cared for you, to give **them permission to care for you!**

It's your turn. Since you are an adult the only person who can give permission for *you* to care for *you* is… *you*.

The way to achieve balance in your life now is for YOU to give yourself permission to set some boundaries that are self-honoring. Boundaries are lines you don't allow people to cross. You have a right to determine lines that are not to be violated; lines that are deal-breakers for you. An example of a boundary line may be: no one is ever allowed to verbally, emotionally or physically abuse you. Ever. Period. That can be a boundary that NO one is allowed to cross and retain a friendship with you. Another boundary line may be that of lending money to people who view you as an ATM (and never repay you). Draw a line. Stop the madness and stop lending them money. Decide whether you can afford to *give* money away or not and then be at peace.

Fill in as many **Permission Slips** as are necessary to get your life back into balance:

.... **PERMISSION SLIP** ....

I, *(fill in your name)*_____, being of sound mind do hereby give myself permission to establish boundaries for*_____

_____

_____

_____

_____

_____

(*fill in the issue: lending money; babysitting other people's children; allowing myself to be abused in anyway; cleaning up after grown folks; etc.) This **Permission Slip** is signed by **me**: _____
as of _____ *(month, date, year)*.

....

Remember, you have trained some folk on how to *move* boundary lines so do not be surprised when they don't want you to re-align boundaries in a healthy and balanced way. Hold your ground in a loving yet firm manner.

P.S. You must have this **Permission Slip** signed in order to go on the field trip called *The Journey Back to You*.

Your ***Declaration of Independence from Imbalance*** is the next document that will require your authorization. Does this sound familiar:

> We hold these truths to be self-evident, that all men are created equal, that they are endowed by their Creator with certain unalienable Rights, that among these are Life, Liberty and the pursuit of Happiness.

This is an excerpt from the July 4, 1776 unanimous Declaration of the thirteen United States of America. The Congress of the United States had to commit in writing how the government would be run. It's your turn.

Whereas the United States was declaring their freedom from British rule, you have a right to declare your freedom from an imbalanced life.

Several years ago, as I sought the Lord in prayer about imbalances in my own life and the distress that ensued as a result, He shared with me the concept of "right proportion." Using the analogy of baking a cake I clearly heard the Lord explain that a **balanced** cake recipe does not call for equal parts of each of the ingredients. You do not add 1 cup of flour, 1 cup of sugar, 1 cup of eggs, 1 cup of vanilla extract, 1 cup of butter and so on. To bake a cake successfully you add the right ingredients in *right proportion*. Let me repeat this, because I was greatly blessed by this insight: you add the right ingredients in the *right proportions!*

To balance your life you most likely will not be adding 8 hours of work plus 8 hours of sleep plus 8 hours of leisure time plus 8 hours of exercise all in one day. It sounds absurd doesn't it? To balance a particular day you will mix some sleep with some prayer with some work time and some relaxation time. The challenge, as you can imagine, is to have the wisdom to discern and discover the *right proportion* for you in *this* season of your life. Did you hear that: in *this season* of your life because what constituted balance ten years ago or perhaps even this time a year ago may not constitute balance *now*.

As a life coach I have to encourage many of my clients to stop berating themselves for changes (usually decreases) in their energy levels due to changes in their lives such as caring for a newborn or an aging parent. Sometimes they are discounting a significant loss, such as death of a loved-one, which has left them grieving. Suddenly they need more sleep or more time with friends. There is no magic formula for anyone. Your heart of hearts knows what you need. The issue is whether you will quiet your mind to listen to and honor what you hear. Invariably life transitions cost you energy: a new job; marriage; death; divorce; new baby or relocation to a new home. These transitions require energy and to deny yourself the energy and time needed to adjust to the *new reality* is unfair and even mean-spirited. Pause and think about what you need today to balance your life.

Prepare your **Declaration of Independence from Imbalance** by first completing a list of things which create imbalance and wrong proportion, such as:

- Caring too much about what other people will think
- Comparing myself to an earlier version of me: younger age; before I was married; when I had more money; when I lived with my parents; before the demands of this current job or career; before my diagnosis; before I downsized to a smaller place; or _____
- Unrealistic expectations for myself; frustration over the fact that I can't _____
- Other: Imbalance due to _____

Once again I want to encourage you to tell the truth about those changes in your life you may have been minimizing or ignoring that have truly shifted the balance of your reality.

Before you sign your **Declaration of Independence** think about what you need *more of* and *less of*. Here are some considerations for you but please add your own. Do you need more or less of the following:

- Time with others
- Sleep
- Leisure time
- Exercise
- Getting input from others
- Help
- Reflection
- Shopping
- Planning
- Solitude
- Social media interaction
- Time with family
- Hobbies
- Other: _____

Remember, **The Gift of Balance** is all about finding out what constitutes "right proportions" for your life **today** and accepting that you may need something entirely different tomorrow, next week or next year.

..... **DECLARATION** OF **INDEPENDENCE** ....

I, *(fill in your name)* _____, being of sound mind do hereby declare my independence from the imbalances of _____

_____

_____

I am no longer bound or imbalanced. I am free from whatever has held me captive and off balance and I take full responsibility for balancing my life by the **right proportion** of what I know I require. I furthermore hereby commit to **balancing** my life with MORE _____

_____

and LESS _____

_____

_____.

This **Declaration of Independence** is signed by *me*:

_____

as of _____ *(month, date, year)*.

....

STARTING HERE – STARTING NOW

Congratulations! You've opened **10 GIFTS** and engaged in thoughtful self-examination and reflection. You are now ready for the next step in the journey back to a healthier, affirmed, unconditionally loved 'you'. Only three more questions before we move into the prescriptive work of identifying changes you can make **starting here – starting now**.

The first question is: **How have you given too much of yourself away?** Think about your answers or write them in your journal or workbook. After you list specific instances of when you simply went too far, answer question number two: **Could you have said 'No'?** Record your response to each instance you cited. Finally, question number three: **What did giving too much of yourself away cost you?** Did it cost you peace of mind; money, self-esteem, rest, or something else? Sit with what you wrote. If need be, apologize to yourself and promise yourself that moving forward you will do a better job of taking care of you.

Are you ready and willing to choose something else? You have done a lot of soul-searching and truth-telling. Wherever you were when you began this book you have certainly made a U-turn to head back toward the incredible place of wholeness and divine balance.

To complete the journey back to you please make a list of *five* **choices** *(or more)* you are willing to make for yourself, **starting here – starting now**, that add to your happiness, peace, balance, calm and joy: **I now choose...**

1. _____
2. _____
3. _____
4. _____
5. _____

Your five new choices are a starter-list and you are encouraged to add to them. Make a commitment to yourself to follow-thru on your new choices. Be a better steward of this experience called life and remember that your life is not a dress rehearsal – it's the real deal. Your life is a gift regardless of who your parents are or the circumstances of your arrival on the planet. God made you in His image and likeness and calls you His masterpiece. You are full of abilities, potential and purpose. I hope that you will take responsibility for living a happier, balanced, and self-affirming life *starting here and now*.

Here are a seven of my favorite affirmations that you are welcome to speak into your own life:

I am alive for a reason and my life matters.

I celebrate my uniqueness and understand that there is no other person exactly like me in the entire universe!

I am fearfully and wonderfully made.

I am loved without condition and I am learning to love myself the same way!

I establish balance in my life through boundaries.

I have more to give others when I replenish myself; I give out of my overflow.

I am an expression of divine love.

Amen! ▪ *SLWB*

ABOUT THE AUTHOR

Dr. Sheryl L.W. Barnes is an ordained minister of the gospel. She is a teacher, author, speaker, preacher, life coach and CEO of a firm that develops discipleship curricula and instructional materials. Her passion is teaching the Bible so that Disciples of Christ get excited about walking in truth and love. She incorporates drama, improvisational acting, role-play, object lessons, spoken word arts and creative arts.

She holds academic degrees in psychology (B.A.), education (M.A., Ph.D.), philosophy (Ph.D.) and theology (DMin). As an academician she has taught educational psychology, philosophy, ethics and bioethics at the college level. Additionally she has taught the Bible for all age groups and has served as faculty for Ministers-In-Training. She is a sought after retreat facilitator and Bible teacher due to the creative, engaging and experiential methods she uses when teaching the Word by the Spirit of God.

Dr. Barnes is the author of ***Discipleship in the Age of Distraction*** and ***Am I My Sister's Keeper? (Workbook for Teen Girls)***.

She is mother to one adult son and three adult children by marriage. Dr. Barnes and her husband (Linwood) are ministers devoted to advancing the Kingdom of God through their respective mandates.

For more information about Dr. Sheryl L.W. Barnes please visit:
www.sterling-xavier.com

www.ingramcontent.com/pod-product-compliance
Lightning Source LLC
Chambersburg PA
CBHW032059150426
43194CB00006B/579